THE SUTTON LIFE SERIES

Life as a
Battle of
Britain
Pilot

Jonathan Falconer

SUTTON PUBLISHING

Sutton Publishing Limited
Phoenix Mill · Thrupp · Stroud
Gloucestershire · GL5 2BU

First published 2007

British Library Cataloguing in Publication Data
A catalogue for this book is available from the British Library.

ISBN: 978-0-7509-4601-8

Typeset in Bembo.
Typesetting and origination by
Sutton Publishing Limited.
Printed and bound in England.

Life as a
Battle of
Britain
Pilot

Contents

In memory of
Sergeant Kenneth Christopher Holland, RAFVR
Spitfire pilot, 152 Squadron
Killed in action on 25 September 1940 aged 20

Acknowledgements

I am indebted to Wing Commander Peter Ayerst DFC, who flew Hurricanes and Spitfires in the Battles of France and Britain, for his valuable assistance in the preparation of this book; to my friend and colleague Julia Fenn for her constructive criticism of my manuscript; and to Dr Alfred Price, FRHistS, aviation author and historian, for his useful help and advice.

Glossary and abbreviations

Ace	a fighter pilot with five or more enemy aircraft confirmed shot down
Angels	codeword for height in thousands of feet (e.g., Angels one five = 15,000ft)
bale out	to abandon an aircraft in flight
bandit	enemy aircraft
batman	an officer's personal attendant
dispersal	a hard standing or parking area for an aircraft on the edge of an airfield
Flight	an RAF fighter squadron usually has two Flights, named A and B
'g'	the effect of gravity on a pilot, either positive or negative
hp	horse power
in	inches
kill	to shoot down an opponent

GLOSSARY AND ABBREVIATIONS

mm	millimetres
mph	miles per hour
petrol bowser	refuelling vehicle used to replenish aircraft
Rotte	the *Luftwaffe*'s basic fighter formation of two aircraft
R/T	radio telephony
Schwarm	a pair of *Rotten* make up a *Schwarm* (four aircraft)
scramble	the order given to take off and intercept the enemy
section	each Flight on a Squadron is divided into three sections of three aircraft each
Squadron	an RAF formation made up of between twelve and eighteen aircraft
Staffel	or squadron, made up of three *Schwarme* (twelve aircraft)
'V'	or 'Vic', the RAF's basic fighter formation of three aircraft
vapour trail	white condensation trails formed at altitude by condensing hot exhaust gases, usually above 20,000ft
vector	codeword for steering a course in degrees (e.g., vector 090 = steer a course of 90 degrees)

Introduction

Over the years, a great many books have been written and published about the Battle of Britain and its pilots. More than half a century later it is still one of the most keenly debated actions of the Second World War. There are some who believe that the pilots of RAF Fighter Command saved Britain from invasion in the late summer of 1940; there are others who maintain that it was not the RAF who won the Battle of Britain and that its 'finest hour' is nothing but a myth, manufactured by the RAF itself and by the prime minister of the day, Winston Churchill. Others think that it was the powerful presence of the Royal Navy in Britain's coastal waters, which had the power to sink the Nazi invasion armada, that convinced Hitler an amphibious invasion of Britain was too risky.

Whichever point of view you sign up to, the Battle of Britain remains a strategic turning point of the early years of the Second World War. Apart from the most obvious outcome – Hitler's cancellation of his invasion plans – the battle witnessed major changes in tactics: the *Luftwaffe* abandoned its large-scale daylight bombing of Britain in favour of night raiding, and RAF Fighter Command went on to the offensive, flying fighter sweeps into continental Europe.

The Battle of Britain was important in a number of other ways. It was one of the first major battles to be reported in 'real time' by the BBC and the press. It also saw the RAF become the news media's darling, a position it occupied for much of the war.

In the summer of 1940, as far as the British public was concerned, the RAF meant fighter pilots. The words 'Royal Air Force', 'Spitfire', 'Hurricane' and 'fighter pilot' were uttered reverently almost every-where across the land, from tasteful suburban draw-ing rooms and country cottages, to smoky public bars and on London's crowded tube trains.

If the Battle of Britain gave the RAF its public image, it was its young fighter pilots who gave it a human face. So, who were 'the Few' and where did they come from? What aircraft did they fly? How did an RAF fighter pilot spend a typical day? What clothing did he wear? And what did he do at 30,000ft over Kent when his squadron clashed with swarms of German Messerschmitts?

In the following pages you will discover what it was like to be an RAF fighter pilot in that fateful summer of 1940. When you have finished reading, ask yourself, 'would I have been up to the job?'

Jonathan Falconer
Bradford-on-Avon
15 September 2006

Prologue

Southern England: an early morning
in the late summer of 1940

A patchy ground mist drapes Kent's gently rolling fields and woodland, its translucent chill wrapping their soft contours in a clammy mantle. The sun has been up for a couple of hours, but its warming rays have yet to burn off the lingering mist. A piercing azure sky arches overhead, clear and cloudless. Empty. All is still. Another hot day beckons. Within hours the rattle of machine guns and the scream of aircraft locked in air battle will shatter the calm; the vigorous tracery of aircraft vapour contrails will describe life and death struggles high in the blue overhead.

If you were to climb into a fighter plane now before this deadly aerial ballet unfolds and skim over the sleeping woodlands, buzz at cornstalk height across the scratchy yellow stubble and then gently pull back on the joystick to lift your aircraft over and beyond the criss-cross lattice of hedgerows in the far distance, there you would find an aerodrome. It is one of several dozen in this beautiful corner of England. Being a grass field it is relatively well hidden, but with its supporting infrastructure it is still a man-made intrusion into this rural idyll. Here can be found men and machines, guns and bullets, a determined hive of activity with a grim purpose. Two squadrons of Spitfire fighters are stationed here, with hundreds of men and women to look after and service them, and a handful of eager young men to fly them into battle when the time comes. It is the Battle of Britain. The nation is at war with Germany, and has been for a year. Britain is fighting for its survival.

The Prime Minister, Neville Chamberlain, announced the declaration of war in a sombre broadcast to an expectant but stunned nation, huddled around their wireless sets, on 3 September 1939. Since then Britons puzzled over the 'phoney war' when nothing much seemed to happen, but with the spring of 1940 came the hurried withdrawal of British forces from Norway and the unleashing of the Nazi *blitzkrieg* on France and the Low Countries. It culminated in the humiliating evacuation of the British Expeditionary Force from the beaches of Dunkirk in May. With Hitler's unstoppable armies massing on the shores of northern France to strike across the Channel, it seemed just a matter of time before Britain fell.

The fate of the nation depended on the *Luftwaffe* destroying the RAF and gaining mastery of the skies to enable its paratroops and seaborne invasion armada to land along the south coast. If they gained a toe-hold and were not thrown back into the sea by the defenders, then the Germans would become the first foreign power to invade Britain's shores since the French under William of Normandy at Hastings in 1066.

In June 1940, Winston Churchill, the new prime minister of Britain's wartime coalition government, recognised the grave danger the nation faced. In a memorable speech to Parliament he told how Britain stood alone and that the fate of the nation, and indeed the free world, now hung in the balance. Britain was fighting for its very survival and it was just a matter of weeks before Hitler's invasion armada was expected to set sail across the Channel. All that lay between invasion and freedom was the professionalism and determination of a small band of RAF fighter pilots, their Spitfires and Hurricanes. In a pitched air battle that raged over southern England in the high summer and autumn of 1940, the thin blue line of RAF Fighter Command succeeded in routing a numerically superior enemy force and turned the tide of fortune, forcing Hitler to shelve his plans to invade Britain.

As a prelude to the invasion, codenamed Operation *Seelöwe* (Sealion), the Germans launched a series of air attacks against Britain, first against coastal shipping mainly in the Channel and along the southeast coast of England, then against the RAF's airfields, its radar stations, aircraft and pilots. Just when Goering's strategy of destroying the RAF on the ground was coming close to success and Fighter Command near to breaking point, Hitler ordered a sudden change of tactics. Instead of the destruction of the RAF, he now wanted London bombed and its inhabitants blasted into submission. The Führer had inadvertently given Fighter Command the vital breathing space it needed; and his tactical blunder marked the turning point in the battle.

The climax came on 15 September when the *Luftwaffe* planned to engage the dwindling numbers of defending RAF fighters and their pilots while simultaneously raining tons of bombs onto London. The outcome was not the defeat of the RAF and the destruction of civilian morale that Hitler expected, but a serious mauling of the *Luftwaffe*, which lost fifty-six aircraft for the RAF's twenty-seven (from which fourteen pilots were safe). As one commentator put it, 'London burned; but Britain was saved.' Two days later, Hitler announced that the invasion of Britain had been postponed indefinitely.

Officially, the Battle of Britain is said to have begun on 10 July and ended on 31 October 1940 – 107 days of intense air combat. But those who did the attacking, namely the *Luftwaffe*, dispute these dates. The major round of daylight assaults had ceased by the end of October, but the battle was far from over and the *Luftwaffe* continued to attack Britain by day and night until May 1941.

The reason the Air Ministry chose those dates was because they thought of the battle as a campaign. For fighter pilots and other aircrew of RAF Fighter Command to qualify for the award of the Battle of Britain clasp to a campaign medal, there had to be a qualifying period for such an award – in other words, a beginning and an end date. Thus, the time between 10 July and 31 October 1940 was chosen, and this is how it has come to be regarded as marking the official duration of the Battle of Britain.

Overlooked by many accounts of the Battle of Britain is that the two other operational Commands of the RAF (Bomber and Coastal) materially aided the campaign by bombing German war industry, airfields and port facilities, and the massed invasion barges in the Channel ports. There was also the presence of the Royal Navy – then the most powerful navy in the world – in Britain's coastal waters, which posed a real and potent threat to any German invasion armada should it ever have set sail. If RAF Fighter Command played the leading part in the epic drama of the Battle of Britain, then Bomber and Coastal Commands and the Royal Navy played the vital supporting roles.

CHAPTER 1

Squadron Scramble!

*A day in the life of an RAF Battle of Britain
fighter pilot*

*You single out an opponent. Jockey for position. All clear behind!
The bullets from your eight guns go pumping into his belly.
He begins to smoke. But the wicked tracer sparkles and flashes
over the top of your own cockpit and you break into a tight turn.
Now you have two enemies. The '109 on your tail and your
remorseless, ever-present opponent 'g', the force of gravity.*

**Flying Officer Johnnie Johnson,
19 Squadron, September 1940**

R esponsibility for the defence of Great Britain
from air attack falls upon the men and
machines of RAF Fighter Command. Thanks to a

chain of long-range radar stations sited at strategic points around the coast, incoming enemy aircraft can be detected up to 100 miles away, and their movements plotted. This means that instead of a handful of RAF fighters having to maintain standing patrols all day long, they can be waiting on the ground at immediate readiness. When a suspect plot is seen on the radar screens, Spitfires and Hurricanes can be scrambled to intercept the incoming raid, with their fuel tanks full and the pilots in good shape for a fight.

The daily routine of a front-line RAF fighter squadron during the Battle of Britain varies very little. For a job that is perceived by many as glamorous, the start of the day for an RAF fighter pilot is anything but. His batman rouses him from sleep at about 4 a.m. as dawn is breaking, and his day will not end until the squadron is stood down again at about 8 p.m. If he is an officer, his batman will thrust a mug of steaming hot tea or cocoa into his hand (a sergeant pilot will have to find it for himself), then he hurriedly washes and dresses before joining the other pilots outside the billet in the half-light of dawn to wait for transport out to the dispersals. These can be up to a couple of miles away.

Out at the dispersals the fitters are busy running up the Rolls-Royce Merlin engines of their charges and completing the scheduled daily inspections. Three ground crew men are allocated to each Spitfire or Hurricane: a fitter who looks after the engine; a rigger who deals with the airframe; and an armourer who is responsible for the eight machine guns. When their tasks are completed the bellowing engines are cut and silence returns. It is then the turn of the refuelling crews in their waiting petrol bowsers to top up the aircraft fuel tanks with 100-octane petrol – 85 gallons per aircraft.

At the flight dispersal area the pilots, if they are on a permanent station, wait in the readiness hut, in a tent if at a satellite airfield, or simply lying on the grass or lounging in deckchairs, for the inevitable call to action. Their flight commander has already telephoned through to Operations to say they are ready for business. The tedium and tension of waiting now begins. Pilots spend their time reading the popular magazines of the day such as *Lilliput* or *Picture Post*, playing card games and darts, or just smoking cigarettes and contemplating what the day will hold. Tiredness and tension are great conversation stoppers.

An officer with the rank of squadron leader commands a fighter squadron, which is made up from two Flights, named A and B, each of which is commanded by a flight lieutenant. Each Flight is divided into three sections, Red, Yellow and Green, each of which has three aircraft, for example Red One, Two and Three.

One section at a time leaves the dispersal for breakfast for no more than 20 minutes, with the same arrangements for lunch and tea, although these meals are invariably alfresco snacks – a mug of soup or a corned beef sandwich hurriedly consumed beside the aircraft or in the shadow of a wing.

Air Chief Marshal Sir Hugh Dowding, the Commander-in-Chief of RAF Fighter Command in 1940, had hoped to allow each of his squadrons one day's rest a week, but as the battle gathered pace and the situation became ever more desperate, this was not always possible for his hard-pressed pilots.

As the sun rises higher in the sky, the air temperature rises with it, and so too does the tension among the waiting pilots. The highly charged atmosphere of nervous expectation at the dispersal is almost palpable. For some, the seemingly interminable waiting plays havoc with their stomachs. The sound of a telephone ringing in the readiness hut is enough to send a man lurching behind an aircraft to throw up the contents of his knotted stomach; such is the high level of anticipation. When the call to action finally comes it's with a metallic click of the microphone switch echoing through the tannoy, or the tinkling of a telephone bell that heralds the frantic call of 'Scramble, scramble!'

The fitters press the starter buttons on their battery carts that provide the power via a cable to start the engines. The propellers turn over and whirl into life, and gouts of yellow flame followed by clouds of sooty smoke issue from the exhaust stubs of the aircraft, as the pilots sprint across the grass to their waiting machines. They grab their parachute packs off the wings or the tailplanes, where they have been placed earlier for convenience, and clip them on. Climbing up on to the wing root, the pilot lowers himself into the close confines of the cockpit, straps in, pulls on his flying helmet and connects his intercom lead and oxygen supply. The ground crew disconnect the battery plug and slam shut the flap on the aircraft's nose. As the ground crew stand clear the pilot gives them the thumbs up, pushes open the throttle and his aircraft begins to roll across the grass.

The little fighter snakes forward. Even with the canopy locked back and the cockpit seat cranked up as high as it will go to enable him to see ahead around the long nose, the pilot still finds it difficult to see where he is going. Rolling faster across the grass now, the fighter bobs and bounces its way forward until the tail rises and soon the plane becomes airborne.

When still only feet above the ground the pilot nips the brake lever on the control column several times to stop the two main wheels turning. On the Spitfire, he manually retracts the undercarriage using the big hydraulic handpump lever inside the cockpit to his right, taking care not to rasp his knuckles on the side of the cockpit. Pumping away with his right hand, his left hand grasps the yoke of the control column and involuntarily 'pumps' as well, rocking the column back and forth; it is not unusual to see a Spitfire 'porpoising' on take-off. The pilot raises the twin legs into their wheel wells beneath the wings, lowers his seat and slides closed the cockpit canopy before his section joins the formation of squadron fighters climbing at full throttle to gain height – the all-important advantage when finally facing the enemy.

Crackling through on the formation leader's R/T headphones come the clipped tones of the ground-based fighter controller in the sector operations room, many miles away and several thousand feet below: 'Lorag leader, vector two three zero, bandits one hundred plus, angels two zero.' This is the shorthand language of the airman which, translated, means: 'leader of 242 Squadron, steer a course of 230 degrees where you will find more than one hundred enemy aircraft at a height of 20,000ft.'

Climbing to altitude with the rest of his squadron to intercept the incoming enemy formation, the pilot repeatedly scans the sky around and behind him for signs of the intruders, while all the time maintaining a running check on the cockpit instruments and engine settings. Nimble fingers constantly adjust the control settings to enable the fighter to keep station with the others in the formation.

One of the squadron's pilots spots the tell-tale vapour trails of the enemy soaring above. He radioes his formation leader to tell him. Closer inspection might reveal Heinkel He111 or Junkers Ju88 bombers with a protective screen of Messerschmitt Me109 or Me110 fighters weaving above them, pulling long white vapour trails against the deep blue sky. Now that the enemy finally has been sighted, the pilot's stomach knots again and his pulse quickens with the sudden adrenalin rush ahead of the fight to come. The leader orders the squadron into the attacking formation practised many times before, but now it is for real. As they climb at full throttle towards the enemy, the pilot runs his final cockpit checks to make sure the oxygen supply is turned 'on', the reflector sight is turned to the 'bright' position, and that the gun button is set to 'fire'.

When battle is joined it is every man for himself. Survival depends on keeping a cool head, anticipating the next move of your opponent (who is as hell bent on his own survival as you are on yours, and who is out to kill you too), keeping a sharp lookout all around and last, but certainly not least, good marksmanship. Luck also plays a vital part in survival because if you are in the wrong part of the sky at the wrong time, all the skill and judgement in the world won't save your skin.

Dogfighting exacts a fearsome toll from the frail human body and its senses. The pilot often flies at heights of 30,000ft, with no cockpit heating or pressurisation, and without the benefit of any special protective flying clothing. With the 12-cylinder Rolls-Royce Merlin engine running at full power a matter of feet in front of him, the din in the cockpit is terrific, pounding the eardrums incessantly. With the enemy in his sights the pilot thumbs the 'fire' button on the control column, and the whole aircraft shakes from the rattle of the eight Browning machine guns in the wings as they pump bullets into their quarry at the rate of 13lb of shot every 3 seconds. Tight turns at high speed, in dives and climbs, can cause the pilot to black out momentarily when the high gravity loadings experienced – sometimes up to 6 'g' (or six times the force of gravity) – drain blood from the brain. And with no power-assisted controls in a Spitfire or Hurricane, throwing a fighter aircraft around the sky is an arm-aching and sweaty business. The pilot has to summon every ounce of his physical strength to maintain control against the huge elemental forces acting on the control surfaces. It is indeed a hostile environ-ment – both inside the cockpit and out.

Combat might last no more than 10 minutes, amid a sky swarming with aircraft, all wheeling and jostling to get a bead on their quarry, or trying to shake off an attacker clinging to their tail. A pilot has about 3 seconds to identify his adversary before

bringing his guns to bear at less than 250yd range –
and a little longer to abandon his fighter if he is hit.
This is all achieved without the benefits of radar and
electronic gadgetry that are commonplace in fighter
cockpits of the twenty-first century.

Then all of a sudden a pilot might find himself
alone in the big blue arena of the sky with no one in
sight for miles around. The battle has moved on.
Running low on fuel and with his guns out of
ammunition, he is a sitting duck if he sticks around
any longer, so it is time to return to base.

Back at the aerodrome, the pilot files a combat
report with the intelligence officer. It records full
details of his sortie: what happened, where and
when; if he was involved in a dogfight, whether it
resulted in damage to the opponent, or the aircraft
was seen to explode in mid-air or to crash. If this is
the case, it will be claimed as a 'kill'. A pilot needs to
score five confirmed kills before he can join the elite
band of fighter aces.

When the squadron's lucky pilots begin to arrive back in ones and twos after combat, the headcount begins. Some have landed away at other aerodromes, or have been forced down in a convenient field, because of fuel shortages or battle damage; others may have successfully baled out after their fighters were crippled in combat. A phone call to the squadron later in the day will eventually set minds at rest that they are safe and not 'missing in action'. Then there are the others who will never come back.

The unlucky ones invariably met their end in fear and pain, and, worst of all, alone. Some may have been shot down in action, crashing into the sea or piling vertically into the ground at high speed. They may still have been alive when the sea closed over them, or when they smashed into the earth. Others were burned alive in their cockpits when the petrol tanks in front of them ignited and exploded. Some pilots who had managed to bail out of their stricken fighters were machine-gunned in mid-air by

German pilots as they hung defenceless from their parachutes. Those who cheated death but suffered serious injury might spend many months in hospital recuperating. There were others who sustained injuries of a different kind, their horrific combat experiences scarring their minds so deeply that their lives thereafter became a waking nightmare.

For pilots who suffered serious burns, their hands and faces were skilfully rebuilt by the pioneering plastic surgeon Archibald McIndoe at East Grinstead Hospital. The techniques of this new branch of surgery were in their infancy in 1940, and, as a result, the men who placed their trust in the hands of this brilliant surgeon were known affectionately as 'McIndoe's guinea pigs'.

Back at the aerodrome the pilot may fly another two or three sorties, which can be standing patrols or interceptions. Once again he is likely to encounter the enemy and engage him in combat. As the day wears on, fatigue steadily overcomes him until he is finally stood down in the early evening. Physically and mentally exhausted, he might eat a hurried supper, then return to his quarters and collapse into bed before sinking into an uneasy sleep. If he has a scrap of energy remaining, a trip to the local pub to unwind with fellow pilots over a few pints and a game of darts is a welcome break from the action of the day.

It's a strange existence, this double life of a fighter pilot. In the early morning he might be sitting on the edge of his bed sipping cocoa and contemplating the day ahead; by lunchtime he could be fighting for his life at 30,000ft over Kent in his Spitfire against a horde of Me109s. By the evening, if he survives, he might well be drinking ale with the locals in an English country pub.

The next day a similar pattern is repeated, beginning at 4 a.m. And so the daily battles with the *Luftwaffe* continue, day by day, until well into the autumn. By then the pressure on Fighter Command and its pilots is beginning to ease.

CHAPTER 2

Who were 'the Few'?

*And what did it take to become an
RAF fighter pilot?*

*Let us not forget how a handful of young men – surely the most
highly skilled that we have ever known in the profession of the
bearing of arms – stood as a bastion, and they rendered to the
free world a service for which we should be eternally grateful.*
**Air Chief Marshal Sir Hugh Dowding, Air Officer Commanding-
in-Chief, RAF Fighter Command, 1940**

In a famous and oft-quoted speech to Parliament
on 20 August 1940, Winston Churchill voiced his
admiration for the RAF and its fighter pilots in
particular when he proclaimed that 'Never in the

field of human conflict was so much owed by so many to so few.' It was not long before 'the few' was seized on by the press and became the popular – but respectful – collective noun for the RAF's Battle of Britain fighter pilots. It is still used today when people refer to these brave men.

The average member of the British public in 1940 thought of the typical RAF fighter pilot rather as we view the stereotypical rugby club member of today – British, carefree, out for a good time, and able to put the beers away on a Saturday night on the town with the lads. With a few exceptions, nothing could have been further from the truth. Wartime flying, especially in combat piloting a 350mph fighter aircraft like the Spitfire or Hurricane, was a serious business that required a cool head and a steady, calculating nerve. Only a fool would treat it casually because if he did, very soon he would find trouble, jumped by an Me109 – another name recalled on Remembrance Day.

The average age of an RAF fighter pilot in 1940 was about 20 years. Some were as young as 18, and there were others who were aged 30 or more. With the age of majority set at 21, many of the RAF's Battle of Britain pilots were considered too young to vote; but not too young to lay down their lives for king and country.

Not all were British. In fact the RAF's fighter squadrons of 1940 were fairly cosmopolitan in their mix. There were Poles (141), Czechs (87), Belgians (24) and Free French (13) who swelled the ranks, many having escaped across the Channel to England when the Nazis overran their homelands. These men were widely regarded as enthusiastic and fearless fighters with a burning desire to have a crack at the *Luftwaffe*. However, difficulties with language occasionally caused command problems in the air. From farther afield came pilots from the Dominion and Commonwealth countries of Australia (21), New Zealand (129), Canada (90), South Africa (22) and

Rhodesia (2), eager to join their British compatriots in the fight against Nazism. To some extent the influx of men from these countries was thanks to the RAF's reputation for being the 'best flying club in the world'. Before the war there had been a concerted recruitment drive in New Zealand in particular, which resulted in a disproportionately large number of aircrew from this relatively small Dominion coming to England to join the RAF. Canada contributed a substantial number of aircrew, many of whom had signed on with the RAF before the war. There were also men from Palestine (1), Jamaica (1), the United States (7) and Ireland (9), whose belief in freedom and democracy, or simply a desire for adventure, prompted them to travel from afar to join the RAF as fighter pilots in 1940. From closer to home, two Fleet Air Arm squadrons operated under Fighter Command control during the battle, as well as twenty-five naval pilots who were seconded to RAF squadrons.

Roughly two-thirds of the RAF pilots who flew in the Battle of Britain were officers, the other third being sergeant and flight sergeant pilots. Most of these pilots were what was known as short service commission officers (predominantly pilot officers and flying officers), or volunteer reservists (both officers and sergeant pilots). The differences between these categories of pilot are explained below.

In 1940, a pilot officer could expect to earn at least £264 per annum (the equivalent to £31,500 today), a sergeant pilot £226 (equivalent to £26,900). Pay went up by yearly increments to something close to the bottom rate of the rank above (£331 and £273 respectively). Both officer and NCO aircrew also received 'flying pay', which was a small bonus payment, made in recognition of their aircrew status.

All pilots in the RAF of the twenty-first century are commissioned officers; sergeant pilots are a thing of the past in the Service. The RAF in 2006 pays a newly qualified aircrew officer, with the rank of pilot officer, £30,950 per annum, plus a daily flying pay allowance. So the equivalent salary today is not that different from that of 1940.

Most RAF pilots before the war were officers and had joined the Service from public or grammar school backgrounds. A small number who had graduated from the RAF College, Cranwell, were granted permanent commissions in the RAF, which meant they spent their entire working life in the Service. Most, however, entered the RAF on short service commissions that gave them up to five years with the regular Air Force and then four years on the Reserve.

To give the regulars some back-up in case of emergency, a civilian reserve was formed in the shape of the Auxiliary Air Force (AAF) in which all the pilots had commissions and came from middle- and upper-class backgrounds and occupations. The AAF trained air and ground crews at weekends and annual camps, which earned them the nickname of 'weekend warriors'. By 1939 it comprised twenty-one squadrons. One fighter squadron in particular, No. 601 (County of London) Squadron, was known as the 'millionaires' mob' because it had been formed by a group of wealthy aristocrats who also enjoyed membership of an exclusive West End gentleman's club. They showed scant regard for the rigid discipline of the regular Air Force and flaunted their exclusivity by wearing blue ties rather than black, and lining their service tunics with bright red silk. On the outbreak of war, the AAF was subsumed into the RAF and its squadrons became normal RAF line squadrons.

Another source of manpower was the University Air Squadrons (UAS), raised at Oxford and Cambridge Universities in 1925, and at London University in 1935. The RAF saw the need to attract intelligent and well-educated recruits, so it set up the University Air Squadrons where undergraduates could learn to fly in their spare time. These men were not members of the Volunteer Reserve, nor were they obliged to join the RAF, but they could join the Reserve if they wished. The RAF provided the aircraft and instructors, and the ground crews for maintenance and servicing. Uniform as such was not worn, but members wore a navy blue blazer with the UAS badge on the pocket and grey flannels. White overalls were worn when flying. Many officer pilots who flew with the RAF in the Battle of Britain had learned to fly with the University Air Squadrons before the war.

The Air Ministry also introduced the RAF Volunteer Reserve (RAFVR) in 1936 as an additional standby pool of trained pilots, with men drawn from a wide variety of middle- and working-class employment backgrounds. All its recruits were enrolled as potential sergeant pilots, but commissions were available for those men who showed the right qualities. All men who entered the Air Force after the outbreak of war in 1939 did so as members of the RAFVR.

When compared with the German Air Force, the *Luftwaffe*, the RAF differed greatly in terms of the educational background of its pilots and the career opportunities it offered. A German pilot was almost always educated at a state school regardless of his social background or financial status, and if he chose to join the *Luftwaffe* then it was as a full-time career.

RAF fighter pilots had one significant psychological advantage over their German adversaries: they were fighting above their homeland to defend it against invasion and protect their way of life. If an RAF pilot was forced to bale out of his Hurricane or Spitfire, then he knew he was over home territory; though if he came down in British coastal waters, he stood a poor chance of being plucked from the drink by the crews of friendly vessels. It was an altogether different story for the German aircrews, because once they had left the shores of France behind them they were in hostile skies all the way to their English targets, and then back again to their bases. They could be attacked by RAF fighters at any point along their route and if forced down were likely to be captured and made prisoners of war. As we will see in Chapter 3, there was also the very real worry about running short of fuel, since no German aircraft in 1940 had been designed with long-range deep penetration operations in mind.

Although the RAF had top quality equipment and highly trained aircrews and ground staff, it was still unprepared for the extreme demands placed on it by the Battle of Britain. The supply of fighter aircraft to RAF squadrons in the battle was a critical matter, but not as serious as the difficulty in finding trained pilots to fly them. Fighter production from the factories increased month by month, and never failed, but combat losses on the squadrons began to overtake production.

RAF pilots of the late thirties and early forties had learned to fly in single-engine training aircraft like the Tiger Moth biplane, Miles Magister and North American Harvard monoplanes. None of them gave much of a taste of what it would be like to fly high performance monoplane fighters like the Spitfire or Hurricane, though the Harvard came closest. Before joining a front-line fighter squadron from flying training school, newly trained fighter pilots were rushed through an operational training unit in three weeks and arrived on the squadrons with as little as 10 hours' flying experience on type. They were generally much less experienced than the pilots they replaced.

Throughout much of the battle, the output of newly trained pilots from the flying training schools and operational training units failed to keep pace with the casualties on the RAF's front-line fighter squadrons. Needless to say, without trained pilots to fly them, the RAF's Spitfires and Hurricanes were just expensive pieces of machinery sitting on the ground, with nothing to do and nowhere to go.

The *Luftwaffe* attacks during August on Fighter Command's southern airfields and the vital fighter sector stations protecting London were not succeeding. Then, at the point when these attacks could have started to really bite, the *Luftwaffe* made a tactical blunder when it switched its bombing attacks to London. Even so, the pressure on Fighter Command's pilots was still great, and by the opening week of September the RAF's fighter squadrons had on average only sixteen operational pilots each out of their full complement of twenty-six. The *Luftwaffe* was also suffering unsustainable losses. In fact they were losing men and aircraft at about the same rate as the RAF, pro rata.

Tough though it was for Londoners, the *Luftwaffe*'s decision to switch its attention away from the RAF's airfields to bombing the capital gave instant and much needed relief to hard-pressed Fighter Command. It also enabled the production of Spitfires and Hurricanes to outstrip losses again, and, perhaps most important of all, helped replenish the reservoir of trained pilots.

CHAPTER 3

Fighters for 'the Few'

RAF fighter aircraft and their Luftwaffe
adversaries

I flew both Spitfires and Hurricanes. It was like comparing a thoroughbred racehorse with a brewer's dray, a great big brute. The Spitfire was faster. Better rate of climb. Very nimble to the controls – responded quickly. A very beautiful aeroplane. The Hurricane was much larger, more sluggish on the controls.

Squadron Leader Bob Stanford-Tuck, CO 257 Squadron,
September 1940

In 1940, if you were to ask the 'man in the street' to name the RAF fighter aircraft that was winning the air battle against the *Luftwaffe*, he would have said without hesitation 'a Spitfire!' But the reality was somewhat different. Although the Spitfire quickly acquired legendary status as the epitome of Britain's gallant lone stand against the might of the *Luftwaffe*, it did not – and could not – win the battle alone.

Most RAF fighter pilots of 1940 flew one of two principal interceptor fighters in combat. It was these two single-seat single-engine fighters, the Hawker Hurricane and the Supermarine Spitfire, that forged a historic partnership that effectively won the Battle of Britain. Their main adversary was the German Messerschmitt Me109, another superlative single-seater that was similar in many ways to the Spitfire, but whose angular appearance betrayed its Teutonic origins.

Both the Hurricane and the Spitfire owed their existence to a number of crucial developments during the 1930s that had forced the pace of aeronautical change. These were largely the result of technological innovations inspired by the Schneider Trophy series of seaplane races of the 1920s and early 1930s, whose sleek racing machines wowed the cheering crowds of spectators that lined seafronts along the Solent. Britain won the trophy outright in 1931 with its 340.08mph Supermarine S6B racer.

The quest was on for even greater speed and improved engine performance. Aerodynamic streamlining, specialist light aero alloys and metal airframe construction techniques were married to reliable high-power aero engines fed with special fuels. The result was a quantum leap in the development of monoplane aircraft design and engine technology. Without these huge engineering advances, it would have been another ten years before Britain developed the know-how necessary to design and build the Spitfire and Hurricane and the Rolls-Royce Merlin engine that powered both these aircraft – as well as other famous wartime fighters and bombers. Of course, this would have been too late for the Battle of Britain, and probably for the Second World War. Conceivably, it could have cost Britain the war. How different might have been the outcome?

The two RAF fighters were very different in their genesis and appearance: the Hurricane, designed by Sir Sydney Camm, was the logical step in the evolution of Hawker's long and distinguished line of biplane fighters, solid-looking, workmanlike and sturdy. Some observers have likened it to the classic Hawker Fury biplane fighter, but without the top wing and fixed undercarriage. The Spitfire, by contrast, was a work of sheer inspiration. The brainchild of designer Reginald J. Mitchell, it was the first fighter aircraft to be designed and built by the Supermarine company, hitherto renowned for its seaplanes and flying boats. But its fragile, almost dainty, appearance belied a superior performance and hard-hitting firepower that made it a formidable opponent in aerial combat. Although the Hurricane outnumbered the Spitfire by a ratio of roughly two to one in the battle, it was the Spitfire that became the popular symbol of defiance and victory to the British people in the danger that faced them during the invasion summer of 1940.

Much of the burden of the air defence of Great Britain in 1940 was carried by the Hurricane. It was credited with shooting down 656 enemy fighters and bombers against a figure of 529 for the Spitfire. For its time it was an extremely advanced aircraft – a metal- and fabric-skinned monoplane fighter boasting a fully retractable undercarriage, enclosed cockpit and an eight-gun armament. A framed Perspex canopy that slid to the rear afforded the pilot less visibility than from the bulged canopy of the Spitfire. The armament of eight 0.303in Browning machine guns was grouped closely together in blocks of four in the leading edge of each wing, thus giving a good concentration of fire. Powered by a single 1,030hp 12-cylinder liquid-cooled Rolls-Royce Merlin III engine giving a maximum speed of

324mph at 15,650ft, the first Hurricanes entered service with the RAF in December 1937. By the time of *Adlertag* (or Eagle Day) on 13 August 1940, when the *Luftwaffe* launched attacks against coastal airfields and radar stations, the Battle of Britain really got into its stride, and twenty-eight out of the RAF's fifty-five fighter squadrons were equipped with the Hurricane.

The Hurricane was a robust aircraft and a stable gun platform, well able to absorb a huge amount of battle damage such as would have downed the Spitfire or the Me109. Even so, it was inferior in most performance characteristics to the Me109 in its 'E' variant, which was faster and could outclimb and outdive the Hurricane. And with two unprotected fuel tanks in its wing roots, the Hurricane was less likely to make it home after combat than a Spitfire. A more powerful Merlin engine was fitted to the Hurricane from September 1940, giving it an in-creased rate of climb and an improved maximum speed of 342mph at 22,000ft, which made it better able than before to take on the Me109 at high altitude. At low level, though, the Hurricane was more manoeuvrable and could turn inside the '109. In theory, because of its performance shortcomings, Hurricanes more often dealt with the German bomber formations, which tended to fly at about 15,000ft, leaving the faster-climbing Spitfires to engage the higher flying Me109 fighter escort. In the heat of battle things could turn out differently though, and the escorting Me109s often dived down to attack the Hurricanes from above.

Characterised by its beautiful elliptical wing plan form, the Spitfire was the darling of the media in 1940. Similar to the Hurricane, it was a metal-skinned monoplane fighter with a fully retractable undercarriage, enclosed cockpit and a powerful eight-gun armament affording 14 seconds of continuous firing. The Mk I first entered squadron service with the RAF in August 1938, and by mid-August

1940 the type equipped 19 RAF fighter squadrons – which equated to some 326 combat-ready aircraft.

The Spitfire displayed a greater potential for development than its adversary the Me109, and indeed its stablemate the Hurricane. By 1948, Spitfire production had run to 22,758 aircraft in 24 different marks, and 52 operational variants.

A single 1,030hp 12-cylinder liquid-cooled Rolls-Royce Merlin II or III engine powered the Spitfire Mk I, driving a constant-speed variable-pitch propeller, which gave a maximum speed of 355mph at 19,000ft and a maximum diving speed of 450mph. The Mk I could climb to intercept an enemy bomber stream at 20,000ft in 9½ minutes against the 10 minutes that it took for the Hurricane Mk I. By the time of the battle, a constant speed-variable pitch propeller had been fitted which improved both the rate of climb and service ceiling.

The Spitfire was armed with eight 0.303in wing-mounted forward-firing Browning machine guns with 300 rounds per gun, firing outside the propeller arc. Four guns were spread along the leading edge of each wing. A bulged Perspex cockpit canopy gave the pilot better all-round visibility as well as affording him more headroom than in the earlier production models of the Spitfire. The canopy slid to the rear to give access to the cockpit, and a downward-hinged panel on the port side assisted entry and exit.

As already stated, the *Luftwaffe*'s Messerschmitt Me109 single-seat fighter was the main combat adversary of the Hurricane and Spitfire in the Battle of Britain. It could climb and dive faster than the RAF fighters, but in comparison with its opponents the '109's manoeuvrability suffered at high speed when the controls became progressively heavier. The absence of a rudder trimmer meant that the pilot had to work hard with his legs, applying continuous rudder at high speeds in order to fly straight.

The Me109's competitive edge in combat was helped by its direct injection fuel system (in place of a carburettor) that fed fuel to the 1,100hp Daimler-Benz DB601Aa engine. This enabled it to man-oeuvre under negative gravity (or 'g') conditions – for example in a sudden dive – without the engine faltering or cutting out because of fuel starvation. A maximum speed of 336mph at 19,685ft meant it was 19mph slower than the Spitfire, but faster than the Hurricane's 324mph at 15,650ft. Despite these relative differences in maximum speed, rate of climb and manoeuvrability, the Me109E-3 also had the edge on both the Spitfire and Hurricane when it came to the punch delivered by its array of machine guns and shell-firing cannon. It boasted two 7.9mm MG 17 machine guns in the upper decking of the fuselage in the nose with 1,000 rounds per gun, synchronised to fire through the propeller arc, and two wing-mounted 20mm MG FF (Oerlikon) cannon with 60 shells per gun. These cannon had a longer range and greater destructive power than the rifle-calibre Browning machine guns that equipped the British fighters. (The RAF carried out a limited but largely unsuccessful trial with cannon armament on a handful of Spitfires during the battle, but it was not until late 1940 that the first cannon-armed Spitfires began to join the squadrons.)

During the battle the maximum range of the Me109 imposed severe limitations on its fighting capabilities and those of its pilots. The Me109E had fuel for just 20 minutes of actual combat over London, which was at the absolute limit of its effective radius of action. This situation was made worse by orders to escort the slower bomber formations on their way to targets in England, thus wasting valuable fuel.

When it came to the unforgiving arena of air combat, each fighter aircraft possessed some characteristics that were superior to those of its opponent. The Spitfire and Me109 were more evenly matched than the Hurricane and Me109, but the outcome of a dogfight depended to a large extent on the skill of the pilots involved. That said, when Me109 pilots were able to fight without the constraints of range and tactics, the formidable performance and potent armament of the '109 made it, arguably, the best fighter of the battle.

There were two other marques of fighter aircraft in the RAF's inventory during the battle, but neither played such key roles as the Hurricane and Spitfire in its eventual outcome, nor enjoyed much public recognition. They were the Boulton Paul Defiant Mk I, a curious-looking two-seat single-engine fighter with all the armament concentrated behind the pilot in a huge four-gun power-operated turret. As a day fighter it proved a dismal failure. Once the *Luftwaffe's* fighter pilots had got over the initial shock of being shot down by the Defiant's four 0.303in Brownings while making a stern attack, they soon found its Achilles heel. With no forward-firing armament, the turret-armed fighter became easy prey for an enemy fighter pilot mounting a head-on attack, or creeping in below the blind spot to deliver the *coup de grâce*. It was also disadvantaged by the fact that the pilot had to think how to position his aircraft to give the gunner seated behind in his turret the best shot – hardly a good idea when split-second decisions could make the difference between survival and death. The Defiant had the same engine as the Spitfire and Hurricane but, being a two-seater, it was trying to lug around over a ton of extra weight for the turret and its gunner. Its rate of climb in particular was seriously handicapped as a result. To use the Defiant as a bomber destroyer could have made a lot of sense for the RAF, but this was not to be. The RAF's two squadrons of Defiants were withdrawn from the front line by August after suffering unacceptably high losses. In due course the aircraft was to find its niche for a short while in the night skies over Britain during the Blitz.

The twin-engine three-man Bristol Blenheim Mk IF was the other oddball in Fighter Command's inventory in 1940. Adapted from the Blenheim day bomber version by the addition of a ventral gun pack housing a quartet of 0.303in Browning guns, supplementing a single wing-mounted Browning and a Vickers 'K' gun in a dorsal power-operated turret, the Blenheim was already obsolete as a heavy day fighter by the time of the battle. Its disastrous encounters with the high performance Messerschmitt Me109 over France and Belgium in May and June 1940 quickly showed it to be hopelessly outclassed. Fighter Command's Blenheims were therefore relegated to the night interception of German bombers, and the development of airborne interception radar.

Ranged against the RAF in the Battle of Britain were a trio of *Luftwaffe* twin-engine medium bombers. The Heinkel He111, which suffered increasingly heavy losses as a day bomber owing largely to its inadequate defensive armament, was in process of being replaced in the battle by the faster Junkers

Ju88, which experienced a lower attrition rate. The Dornier Do17 also enjoyed greater performance advantages over the He111, but lacked its bomb-carrying capacity and the speed of the Ju88. All three were considered relatively easy prey by RAF fighter pilots, but not as much as the Junkers Ju87 Stuka dive-bomber. The gull-winged Stuka had achieved notoriety in the Polish and French campaigns, but when it came up against determined fighter opposition over England during the battle, it became an easy kill. As a result, the single-engine Stuka was largely held back from dive-bombing attacks against British targets after 19 August.

The Messerschmitt Me110 long-range heavy fighter was thought to be invincible by the *Luftwaffe* chief, Reichsmarschall Herman Goering. Intended to escort the bomber formations, the twin-engine Me110 was outmanoeuvred by the more agile RAF fighters and as a result suffered catastrophic losses during the battle. The ridiculous situation actually arose where the heavy escort fighters had themselves to be escorted by the Me109s.

In the battle, *Luftwaffe* aircraft outnumbered those of RAF Fighter Command by about four to one. With such overwhelming odds stacked against it the RAF seemed destined to go down fighting, yet by September the tables had been turned and the RAF had the *Luftwaffe* on the run. In the end it was a number of factors that changed a seemingly hopeless situation into a victory. In particular, it was the superior performance of the Spitfire and Hurricane over their German adversaries, combined with the skill and bravery of their pilots, that saved the day for Britain in the summer of 1940.

CHAPTER 4

Flying a Fighter

Strategy and tactics

I shot down 109s when flying Hurricanes, but only when I had the advantage of height. I'd stick my nose down and go for them. But a Hurricane couldn't match the 109 on the same level. I spoke to German pilots after the war and they said 'Hurricanes? We didn't worry about them. It was the Spitfires we worried about.'

Squadron Leader Bob Stanford-Tuck, CO 257 Squadron,
September 1940

In 1940, the hordes of German bombers attacking Britain usually had a formidable fighter escort of Me109s and Me110s to protect them. They would also fly in close formation to give each individual bomber the benefit of protection from their combined defensive firepower. Put simply, the job of an RAF fighter pilot in the Battle of Britain was to separate the enemy escort fighters from the bombers, break up the bomber formations and shoot down as many bombers as possible.

The RAF had one major advantage over its *Luftwaffe* adversaries, and that was its system of ground-based fighter controllers who could commit their forces where and when they were most needed in response to the changing enemy threat, thanks largely to radar. Not only were the RAF's fighter squadrons in two-way radio contact with their ground controllers, their pilots were also able to communicate with each other in the air via their high-frequency TR9D wireless sets.

Air combat in the battle took place at all heights, from 30,000ft all the way down to sea level. Whether on a standing patrol or if scrambled to intercept an incoming enemy bomber formation, a fighter pilot had to keep his wits about him all the time. Flying a fighter aircraft meant he could never relax.

A fighter pilot's survival depended on being alert. Once he became airborne he checked and rechecked his instruments and the sky all around him continually. For an experienced pilot these actions became second nature. His systematic scans of the sky began at the left and the rear, his eyes moving in a careful and deliberate up and down zig-zag pattern, searching the sky from high above to below the horizon, gradually working around until he reached the right and the rear. Then he checked again in the direction of the sun, before beginning the procedure all over again. All the time he was doing this, his roving eyes would dart down into the cockpit every few seconds to check that all was well with the instruments and their flickering needles caged in their glass dials.

During the Battle of Britain, famous fighter ace Squadron Leader A.G. 'Sailor' Malan drew up his

'Ten Rules' for air fighting. They were sound advice and quickly achieved widespread fame throughout RAF Fighter Command. Copies could be found pinned to noticeboards in crew rooms and flight offices. His first rule was to hold fire until you could see the whites of your opponent's eyes, then fire short bursts of 1 to 2 seconds – and only when your gunsight was definitely 'on' the target. He also recommended that pilots should always keep a sharp lookout and never fly straight and level for more than 30 seconds in the combat area. The advice from other experienced pilots was never to stop searching the sky or you would probably end up dead. The enemy that got you was the enemy you never saw – coming out of the sun, or lurking in your blind spot.

With so much at stake, it was no surprise that a fighter's Perspex cockpit hood had to be kept spot-lessly clean and transparent. Perspex was a very fragile plastic material and needed to be treated with care. The slightest abrasion caused scratches that made light scatter off the hood. Before a sortie the ground crew would carefully polish the Perspex with a soft cloth to remove any smearing caused by dirt or oil. A tiny speck of dirt could mask the presence of an enemy fighter closing in for the kill, with potentially devastating results.

RAF fighter aircraft of this period were not equipped with heated cockpit hoods or windscreens, which meant that the cockpit glazing could easily become frozen over at altitude. Hoar frost could appear on the inside of the cockpit hood as a result of the intense cold, and in a dive the inside of the windscreen often became covered in ice. In such conditions it was then impossible to see forwards or upwards, and, as fast as a pilot wiped away the ice, more formed. A pilot would therefore be unable to lay his gunsight on his quarry through the windscreen, so he would have to beat a hasty retreat away from any action. When his fighter reached denser and more humid air at a lower altitude, the ice turned to mist so he was kept hard at it rubbing his gloved hands over the cockpit glazing and instruments to keep small patches free from condensation.

The fighters of both sides in the battle were fitted with reflector gunsights. Early Spitfires and Hurricanes had been fitted with a simple ring and bead gunsight, but in the battle all were equipped with the Barr and Stroud GM2 reflector sight, which was positioned above the cockpit instrument panel and behind the windscreen. German fighters were fitted with the Revi reflector sight, which was similar.

The Barr and Stroud device was simple but effective, and like the German Revi its big advantage over the ring and bead sight was that it could be used in conditions of poor visibility. The anticipated range – the gun harmonisation distance, or the point ahead at which the gunfire converged – was set on the upper adjusting ring of the sight. Meanwhile, the wingspan dimension of the target aircraft was set on the lower ring. A central dot and horizontal and vertical ranging lines were projected onto an inclined reflector on the sight. When the target spanned the gap between the inner ends of the reflected horizontal lines, the enemy aircraft was in range – fire!

As we have already seen, both the Spitfire and Hurricane were armed with eight 0.303in Browning machine guns fitted in the leading edges of the wings. The Spitfire's guns were spread out with four Brownings along each wing, whereas the Hurricane's were closely grouped in two banks of four along the inboard leading edges. All eight guns were harmonised to converge on a single point in front of the aircraft and cross over at between 250 and 200yd, which meant that an inexperienced pilot thrown into the battle had a chance of hitting something if he got into the correct firing position. The pilot fired the guns by pressing a button on the control column grip, which could give him an uninterrupted rate of fire equivalent to about 1,200 rounds per minute. With only 300 rounds per gun, this meant 14 seconds of fire before running out of ammunition.

In individual combat with the Me109, the Spitfire and the Hurricane could turn inside their adversary whose turning radius was that much greater. This meant that the '109 pilot would be unable to keep the RAF fighter in his sights. If he was an inexperienced pilot or just not careful enough, he could quickly end up with the RAF fighter on his tail pressing home an attack. If jumped from behind, the '109 pilot's response was to push the stick forward and dive away as fast as possible, a defensive manoeuvre made possible by the aircraft's direct fuel injection system to the Daimler-Benz DB601 engine. He would then zoom-climb to gain height and get into position again, ideally with the sun behind him, to make an attack. In 1940, RAF fighters could not follow a '109 down in a dive – their Merlin engines would cut out because the float carburettor that fed the engine with the fuel and air mixture failed to deliver under negative gravity or 'g'.

The cockpits of the Spitfire, Hurricane and Me109 were all fairly cramped. In particular, the Me109 suffered from low headroom when the hood was closed, which caused problems for taller pilots. To compensate for the restricted cockpit height, the pilot's sloped-back seat was placed almost on the floor of the aircraft, with rudder pedals at the same level. This gave a semi-reclining position not unlike a sports car, and actually gave Me109 pilots the edge on their RAF adversaries when it came to their ability to cope with high 'g' manoeuvres in dogfights.

During the Battle of Britain, the kind of tactical formation employed in combat by the RAF's fighter squadrons was considerably inferior to that used by the *Luftwaffe*. Pre-war tacticians saw the RAF fighter as primarily a bomber destroyer, with speed and rate of climb being deemed more important than manoeuvrability. It was also assumed that *Luftwaffe* fighters would not escort their bombers across the English Channel or North Sea when attacking targets in Britain. The Battle of Britain quickly proved the RAF planners' pre-war assumptions wrong.

The RAF taught its fighter pilots to operate in tight formations based on a squadron size of twelve aircraft, divided into four sections of three fighters. They flew in four 'V' formations, with the squadron commander leading the first 'V'. Once the fighters had established visual contact with an enemy bomber formation, the squadron commander led his pilots into position close behind their prey. He then took his own 'V' into attack first, funnelling three banks of eight 0.303in Browning machine guns onto the bombers ahead. Here the RAF fighters stayed until each pilot either ran out of ammunition, his quarry had been shot down, or he himself had been shot down or his engine seriously damaged. Then the section that had been queuing behind that of the commander lined up for its attack once his section had pulled out of the way, and so on until the fourth and final section closed in to deliver its attack.

But these 'by-the-book' tactics would only work in the absence of enemy fighters. In the battle, with large formations of escorting Me109s and Me110s to protect the lumbering bomber streams, it was soon found to be a flawed practice. German pilots dubbed the RAF's 'V' formations '*Idiotenreihen*' or 'rows of idiots'!

By contrast, the basic formation adopted by the *Luftwaffe's* fighters (which proved far more effective than the RAF's outdated tactics) was the *Rotte* of two aircraft, developed in the Spanish Civil War – a tactical formation that is still flown today. Some 200yd separated the pair of fighters, and the responsibility of the number two, or wingman, was to defend his leader from attack. The leader's main role was to attack and shoot down RAF fighters, as well as acting as navigator and cover for his wingman. A pair of *Rotten* made up a *Schwarm* of four aircraft, which flew in a line-abreast formation. A squadron, or *Staffel*, formation of twelve fighters consisted of three *Schwarme* of four aircraft each, stretched out across a mile and a half of sky. The aircraft were loosely spaced both horizontally and vertically, which gave them flexibility and greater ease of manoeuvre. A *Staffel* formation gave *Luftwaffe* fighters the benefit of mutual defensive support and protection from surprise attack, while the RAF's rigid and outmoded tactics placed them at a considerable disadvantage when pitted against the *Luftwaffe* in the battle.

At headquarters of Fighter Command a major dispute quickly blew up over the RAF's fighter tactics, centred mainly on the so-called 'Big Wing' controversy and Air Vice-Marshal Trafford Leigh-Mallory, the commander of Fighter Command's 12 Group. In late August, Leigh-Mallory created a force of three fighter squadrons at RAF Duxford to operate as a single wing formation led by Squadron Leader Douglas Bader, the famous fighter ace who had lost his legs in a plane crash before the war. Several weeks later the wing was increased in size to five squadrons, three of Hurricanes and two of Spitfires.

The idea of the Big Wing was to meet force with force instead of with penny packets of fighters. Scrambled early before the enemy had reached their target, the Wing would intercept the incoming enemy formation in the vicinity of Maidstone and Canterbury. A mass attack by the Wing would ensue and break up the formation, making it easier prey for the paired squadrons of 11 Group. In practice, however, it was never used in this way. Nevertheless, the mere sight of the massed aircraft of the Wing had a powerful negative effect on the morale of the *Luftwaffe*'s fighter and bomber crews.

Leigh-Mallory's Big Wing stood at a moment's readiness to enter the air battles raging over southern

England in 11 Group's area, but it could only do so if invited in by 11 Group and then directed by HQ Fighter Command. The controversy arose because Leigh-Mallory firmly believed that his squadrons had been deliberately excluded from the main action by Keith Park, the commander of 11 Group, and could have been used to far greater effect.

The RAF knew there was a lot wrong with its fighter tactics during the battle, but with the intensity of the fighting in 1940 it was the wrong time to try to change them. When pilots could be in combat three or four times a day, there was simply no time to experiment with new tactics. In any case, newly trained pilots who had been schooled in the older style of close formation flying were joining the squadrons, and it is likely that most would have been incapable of learning a completely new set of tactics overnight.

However, the RAF did attempt to improve the situation in the short term. They widened out the tight formation, allowing pilots to search the sky for the enemy rather than hold an exact position on their leader. And they released a section, or a pair, of experienced pilots to fly a weaving course 1,000ft above and behind the formation, to minimise the chances of a surprise attack from the rear. Together, these measures improved search capabilities and mutual support between pilots, making them better able to engage the *Luftwaffe* on equal terms. It was a lesson that had been learned only just in time.

CHAPTER 5

What did they Wear?

Uniforms and flying kit

It can now be asserted that 'Uniform by Gieves' is not only a hallmark of distinction but has now become a tradition which is firmly established throughout the Services. We extend a special welcome to officers of the British, Dominion and Allied Air Forces.

Advertisement for Royal Air Force uniforms by Gieves

In one of the abiding images of the young men who fought the Battle of Britain, a fresh-faced fighter pilot turns to the camera from the open cockpit of his Spitfire, dressed smartly for combat in his 'best blue' RAF tunic with collar and tie, leather flying helmet and goggles. Today, it would be hard to imagine the pilot of an RAF jet fighter aircraft like the Eurofighter Typhoon wearing such an impractical ensemble of clothing to go to war.

The problem in 1940 was that specialised flying clothing had not kept pace with the huge advances in aircraft design and performance. RAF pilots in the Battle of Britain were flying the very latest fighter aircraft with top speeds of over 350mph, capable of reaching heights of more than 30,000ft, but they were still wearing flying kit designed for the biplane era. It was only in the latter part of the Second World War that better-designed flying clothing and survival equipment became widely available to RAF aircrew.

During the Battle of Britain, RAF fighter pilots went up to fight the *Luftwaffe* in the same clothes they wore in the sergeants' or officers' messes. They usually wore the standard RAF blue service dress uniform that comprised tunic (top button undone – the hallmark of a fighter pilot) and trousers, light blue cotton shirt, detachable collar and black tie, and either a side cap or peaked cap. When flying, their kit generally included leather flying helmet, goggles and oxygen mask, boots, gloves and life-preserver, all worn over the top of their uniform.

Although RAF pilots were issued with full flying kit that often included bulky flying suits, for practical reasons many chose not to wear it; the same went for flying boots. Others, too, often chose not to wear protective gauntlets. In the baking hot summer of 1940, when fighter pilots spent much of their time at 'readiness' on dispersal pans beneath the unrelenting glare of the summer sun, awaiting the call to scramble, to wear thick sheepskin fur-lined flying jackets and bulky leather trousers would have been unbearable. When the order came to scramble, they were expected to race to their waiting aircraft and take off within 2 minutes. Imagine this on a day when temperatures were soaring into the 80s!

Some pilots preferred to fly without their uniform tunic, with shirtsleeves rolled up. Others wore lightweight cotton 'prestige' suits (or overalls) in black, white or dark blue. These were either privately purchased from high-street military outfitters like Gieves & Hawkes, or were leftovers from official RAF issue back in the twenties and thirties. The wearing of such overalls also carried a certain snob value, since it often indicated that the owner was a veteran – a Regular or Auxiliary Air Force pilot, who had been a flier since before the war.

When flying, many pilots removed their starched detachable collars or white roll-neck pullovers and wore a silk scarf or cravat instead, often in their university colours. This was not, as one might have thought, a sign of vanity, but an effective solution to the bane of the fighter pilot's life – chafing and irritation around the neck through perspiration and friction, caused by constantly turning the head to look out for enemy aircraft.

The style and quality of RAF service dress varied greatly and depended on whether the wearer was a

sergeant pilot (a non-commissioned officer) or a commissioned officer pilot. If he was the former, then he
wore an 'off-the-peg' RAF standard issue four-button,
single-breasted blue serge tunic and trousers, with four
pockets, secured around the waist by a belt with a
brass buckle. His flying badge was worn above the left
breast pocket, with sergeant's stripes sewn on each
sleeve, above which at the shoulder was an embroidered cloth RAF albatross badge. If the pilot was a
volunteer reservist, that is, someone who had volun-
teered for service and who was not a career 'regular',
the cloth embroidered 'VR' patches were sewn
beneath the albatross. The coarse woollen serge tunic
and trousers were untailored and itchy, and known to
RAF servicemen for good reason as the 'hairy Mary'.
In winter they were warm to wear, but in summer
they could be unbearably sweaty and uncomfortable.

If you were a commissioned officer, uniform was
altogether a different matter. The tunic and trousers
were beautifully tailored in soft barathea wool, made

to measure by the likes of Allkit or Gieves & Hawkes. In common with its poorer cousin, the 'off-the-peg' standard issue item, it was a single-breasted tunic with four pockets, belted, with the flying badge worn above the left breast pocket, and with braid denoting the wearer's rank stitched around each cuff. If the officer was a volunteer reservist, he wore brass 'VR' insignia on each lapel.

Headwear for an NCO pilot was a standard issue blue serge forage or side cap, with a circular brass RAF badge on the left side. Officers wore tailored peaked caps in blue barathea wool, with a gold bullion embroidered RAF badge at the front. Some removed the wire stiffener from inside the brim, which gave the cap a more crumpled look, indicative of a pilot who had 'got some in'. They could also choose to wear a forage cap in barathea wool, with a brass albatross and crown attached to the left side.

The inevitable class distinctions of the period were much evident in the style and quality of the uniforms worn by sergeant pilot or officer, but flying kit was the great leveller because pilots wore the same equipment, regardless of rank.

Beginning with headgear, the standard flying helmet issued to all RAF aircrew personnel between 1936 and 1941 was the brown leather 'B' Type helmet. Padded and lined with a soft chamois, it was fitted with a leather chinstrap and two domed zipped leather earpieces that housed the all-important radio-telephone (R/T) receivers.

The helmet was worn with flying goggles to protect the wearer from the effects of the elements, fire and flying debris. Most Battle of Britain fighter pilots preferred the simple lightweight glass-lensed Mark II goggles which many pilots still hung on to, despite their being obsolete long before the war began. The alternative was the generally loathed Mark III goggles with their celluloid lenses that were easily scratched, and which impaired vision. Needless to say, in the air-fighting arena you cannot shoot an aircraft down until you see it. With three dimensions in which to look, there's an awful lot of sky to be scanned. Thus, quality of vision could mean the difference between life and death. Because of concerns caused either by a shortage of the favoured Mark II goggles, or a dislike of the Mark III, many pilots were disinclined to wear any goggles at all. This was a decision that undoubtedly led to avoidable casualties in the Battle of Britain as a result of facial burns and serious eye injuries.

In the twenty-first century we take it for granted that we are able to fly in airliners with pressurised cabins at heights of 35,000ft or more without suffering the debilitating effects of extreme cold or oxygen starvation. During the Battle of Britain there were no such things as cabin pressurisation or heating in any aircraft. At heights above 10,000ft pilots and aircrew had to breathe oxygen through a facemask. These masks were made from green Melton wool with a chamois lining and were fitted with a switched microphone for the wearer to talk with other RAF pilots and the fighter controller on the ground. The oxygen mask was clipped to the flying helmet and connected to the aircraft's oxygen supply by means of a flexible hose. Unlike later versions of oxygen supply equipment it was not a 'demand' system, where the life-giving gas only flowed into the mask when the wearer inhaled. For Battle of Britain pilots the oxygen was either 'on' or 'off' and as such was not a very efficient system.

The pilot wore an inflatable life-preserver or life-jacket, also known as a Mae West after the busty Hollywood film star of the period. Pilots usually (and unofficially) painted them with chrome yellow aircraft paint to improve their visibility if they came down in the sea. It had a rubber air bladder that the pilot blew into like a balloon to inflate, and three kapok flotation pads. Pilots were encouraged to wear the life-preserver partially inflated, but attempting to blow it up once in the water might not be particularly helpful or indeed practicable, especially if the wearer was injured or unconscious. On the other hand, a carbon dioxide cartridge automatically inflated the life-preservers worn by their opposite numbers in the *Luftwaffe*, but overall neither buoyancy garment was hugely effective. Both were vulnerable to damage by stray bullets and metal fragments that could render them useless to their wearers.

Life-preservers could only be expected to provide buoyancy for a few hours at the most. To help pilots who were 'down in the drink', inflatable rubber dinghies were issued to prolong their survival until rescuers arrived. Surprisingly, the RAF did not issue its fighter pilots with survival dinghies until after the battle in 1941, although the *Luftwaffe*'s Me109 pilots used single-place life-rafts during its latter stages.

In aircraft as small and compact as a single-seat fighter, there was little room for the pilot to wear a parachute, that vital piece of life-saving equipment if he was forced to 'hit the silk' and abandon his aircraft in flight. The solution was the seat-type parachute where the 'chute pack is attached to the pilot by web straps and a harness, and is then fitted into the pilot's bucket seat in the aircraft, forming a cushion on which he sits. It was then worn (and sat upon) throughout the flight. A pilot's parachute was often left on the wing of the aircraft by the ground crew for the pilot to grab when scrambled. At this point he clipped it on before climbing into the aircraft; or it was ready placed in the cockpit ahead of time. With typical wartime RAF humour, aircrews were often told by the parachute-packing staff to 'bring it back if it doesn't work' for a full refund or replacement!

The footwear of choice for a Battle of Britain fighter pilot was a pair of 1936 pattern calf-length flying boots. Made of sturdy chromed black leather lined with thick pile fleece, the boots were a pull-on style with a tightening strap and buckle at the front.

However, many pilots chose to wear their black leather lace-up dress shoes when flying, since they found flying boots cumbersome in the tight confines of the fighter cockpit. There was another very good practical reason: if they were shot down or baled out, lace-up shoes were more comfortable to walk in to the nearest town or back to base.

Flying gauntlets were supposed to be worn as the outer of four layers of gloves – over pairs of silk and chamois inner gloves, and fingerless woollen mittens – but they seldom were. With a pair of thin metal fuel tanks filled with 85 gallons of highly flammable 100-octane petrol positioned just a matter of feet in front of their faces, it is surprising how many Battle of Britain fighter pilots chose not to wear goggles, gauntlets or boots. Some felt that these items of protective flying clothing impaired their vision and mobility, or reduced their ability to feel the aircraft controls properly. If the volatile fuel in the tanks was set alight by a strike from a bullet or cannon shell, the resulting fire would spread quickly back into the cockpit with the potential to asphyxiate the unprotected pilot and cause him serious – possibly fatal – burns. For those who survived the ordeal, it resulted in painful burns to the hands and face that required many hours of surgery and skin grafts, and a lengthy convalescence.

Since the Battle of Britain, flying clothing and safety equipment have travelled light years in terms of design. Ejection seats, 'g' suits and high-tech 'bone domes' with night vision goggles are now standard equipment for jet-fighter pilots. Developments in computer technology and materials science have made the flying kit of the twenty-first century pilot incomparable with that of his Battle of Britain predecessor.

Epilogue

By the end of October 1940, as far as the RAF was concerned, the Battle of Britain was over. It was the Nazis' first significant defeat since launching their *blitzkrieg* on mainland Europe with the invasion of Poland in 1939. Hitler had called off his invasion of Britain in September to turn his attention towards the East and the conquest of Russia.

The heroes of the hour were undoubtedly the young pilots of RAF Fighter Command. Their skill and bravery against a determined and numerically superior enemy soon became legendary. However, it was the Commander-in-Chief of Fighter Command,

Lord Dowding, who conceived and built the crucial network of Britain's air defences in the 1930s and consequently made victory possible in 1940. It was Dowding who was responsible for saving Britain from invasion.

Both the RAF and *Luftwaffe* suffered heavily in the battle. At the time, in the heat and confusion of the moment, each side filed losses that were greatly overestimated – the British claimed they had shot down 2,698 German aircraft; the Germans believed they had downed 3,058 RAF machines. After 1945, once the dust of war had settled, investigators delved into official records and confirmed the true aircraft losses for the battle were 915 for the RAF, and 1,733 for the *Luftwaffe*. Such is the confusion of war that these wildly extravagant claims were unsurprising. In human terms, this equated to 537 RAF airmen and 2,662 *Luftwaffe* airmen killed.

When confronted with such bland statistics it is all too easy to lose sight of the human tragedy that lies behind them. British or German, they were all young men in their prime who, but for the war, might have lived on into old age.

By the time the Battle of Britain was over, the Second World War had barely begun. The conflict was to last another four and a half years and engulf much of the world in a war that saw more civilians die than combatants. When it finally came to an end in 1945, Nazism and Japanese imperialism had been destroyed. Within years, however, mankind would enter the new dark age of the Cold War and the atomic bomb.

Bibliography

Cross, Roy and Scarborough, Gerald, *Spitfire*,
    London, Patrick Stephens, 1971
—— and Ebert, Hans J., *Messerschmitt Bf109 Versions
    B–E*, London, Patrick Stephens, 1972
Duncan Smith, Group Captain W.G.G., *Spitfire into
    Battle*, London, John Murray, 1981
Forbes, Wing Commander Athol and Allen,
    Squadron Leader Hubert, *Ten Fighter Boys*,
    London, Collins, 1942
Gelb, Norman, *Scramble: A Narrative History of the
    Battle of Britain*, London, Michael Joseph, 1986
Green, William, *Aircraft of the Battle of Britain*,
    London, Macdonald, 1969

BIBLIOGRAPHY

Hough, Richard and Richards, Denis, *The Battle of Britain: The Jubilee History*, London, Hodder and Stoughton, 1989

James, John, *The Paladins: The Story of the RAF up to the Outbreak of World War II*, London, Macdonald, 1990

Mansell, Tony, 'The Origins of Air Crew Who Fought in the Battle of Britain', *Royal Air Force Historical Society Journal*, 36 (2006)

March, Peter R., *The Spitfire Story*, Stroud, Sutton Publishing, 2006

Price, Alfred, *Spitfire at War*, Shepperton, Ian Allan, 1974

Ramsey, Winston G., *The Battle of Britain Then and Now*, London, Battle of Britain Prints International, 1980

Townshend Bickers, Richard, *The Battle of Britain*, London, Salamander, 1990